THE JAZZ CONNECTION

Production: Sadie Cook
Cover Design: xheight design limited

Published 1999

© **International Music Publications Limited**
Griffin House, 161 Hammersmith Road, London W6 8BS, England

Crazy Rhythm

Words by Irving Caesar
Music by Roger Cahn-Wolfe and Joseph Meyer

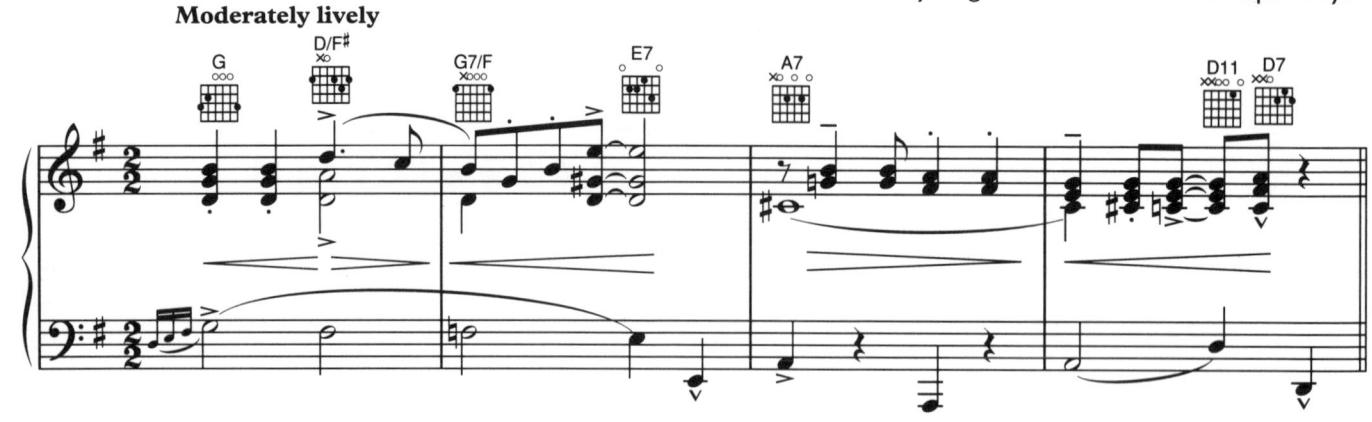

I feel like the Em-per-or Ne - ro when Rome was a ve-ry hot town;
Ev-'ry Greek, each Turk and each La - tin, the Russ-ians and Pruss-ians as well,

Fath-er Kni-cker-bock-er, for-give__ me, I play while your ci - ty burns
when they seek the lure of Man-hat-tan, are sure to come un-der your

Warner/Chappell Music Ltd, London W6 8BS and Redwood Music Ltd, London NW1 8BD

Foggy Day

Music and Lyrics by
George Gershwin and Ira Gershwin

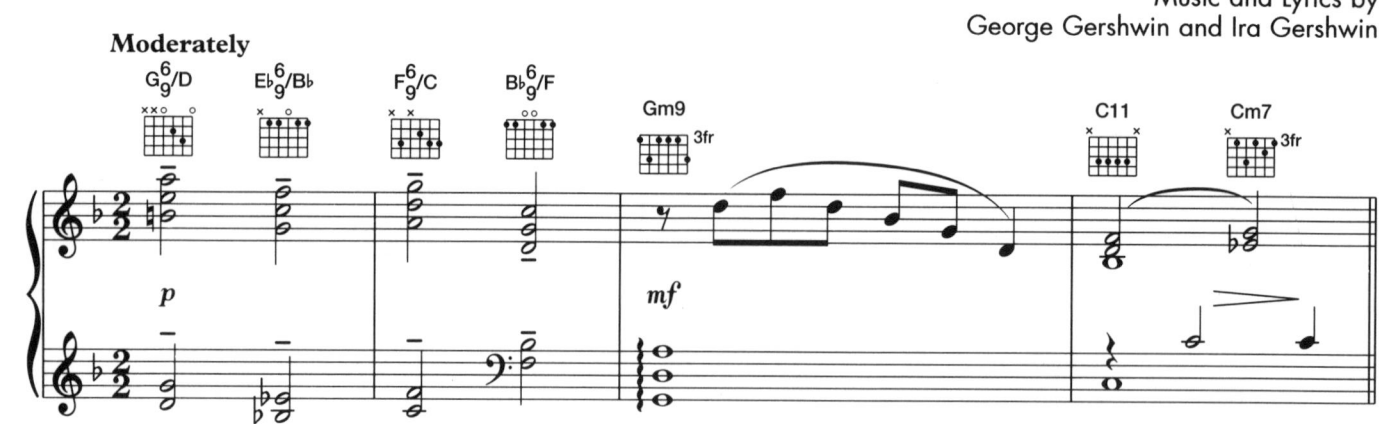

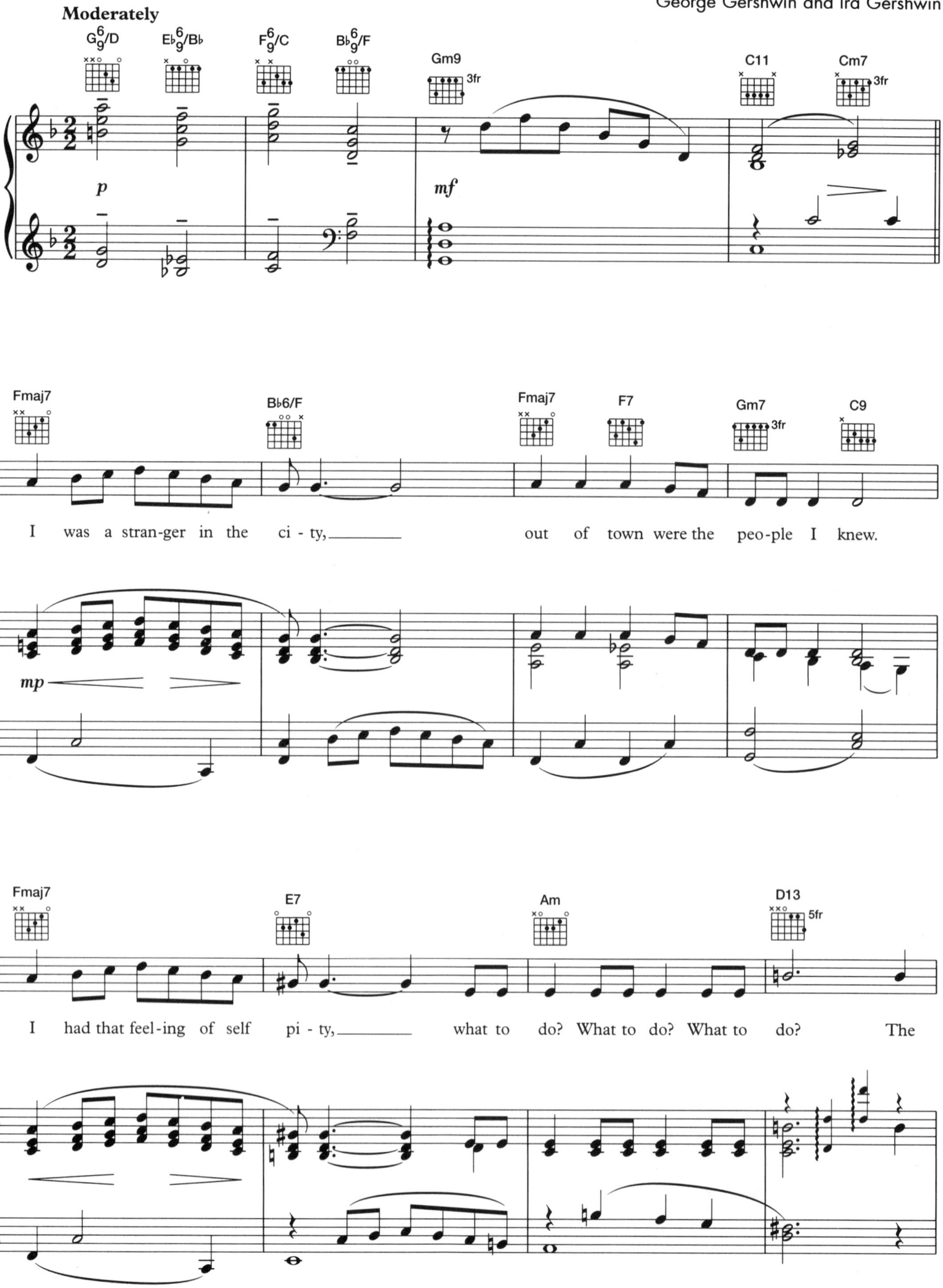

I was a stran-ger in the ci- ty,_____ out of town were the peo-ple I knew.

I had that feel-ing of self pi- ty,_____ what to do? What to do? What to do? The

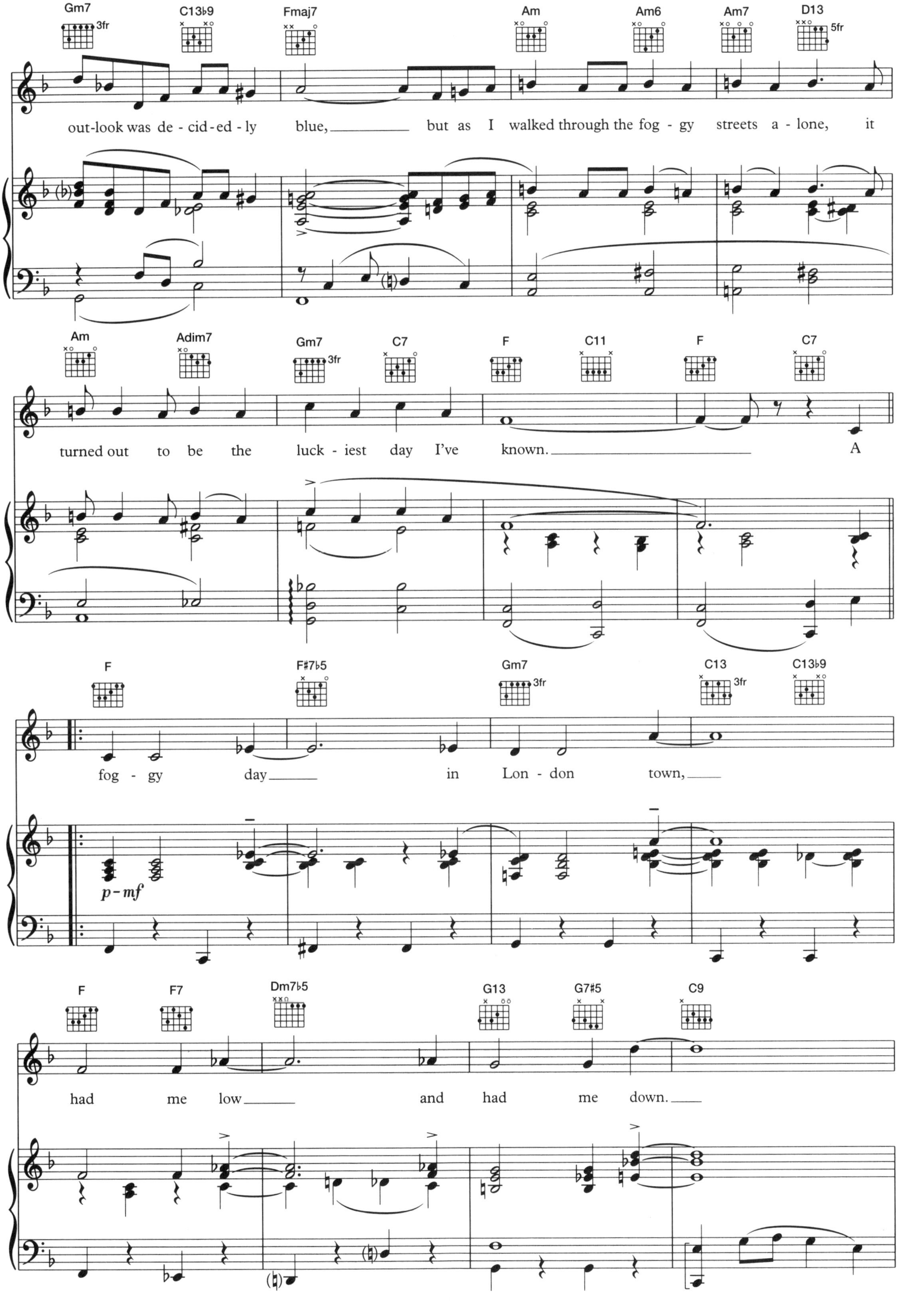
Gm7 3fr C13♭9 Fmaj7 Am Am6 Am7 D13 5fr
out-look was de - cid - ed - ly blue, but as I walked through the fog - gy streets a - lone, it
Am Adim7 Gm7 3fr C7 F C11 F C7
turned out to be the luck - iest day I've known. A
F F♯7♭5 Gm7 3fr C13 3fr C13♭9
fog - gy day in Lon - don town,
p – mf
F F7 Dm7♭5 G13 G7♯5 C9
had me low and had me down.

It Don't Mean A Thing
(If It Ain't Got That Swing)

Words by Irving Mills
Music by Duke Ellington

It's Only A Paper Moon

Words by E Y Harburg and Billy Rose
Music by Harold Arlen

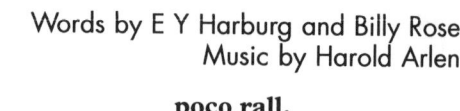

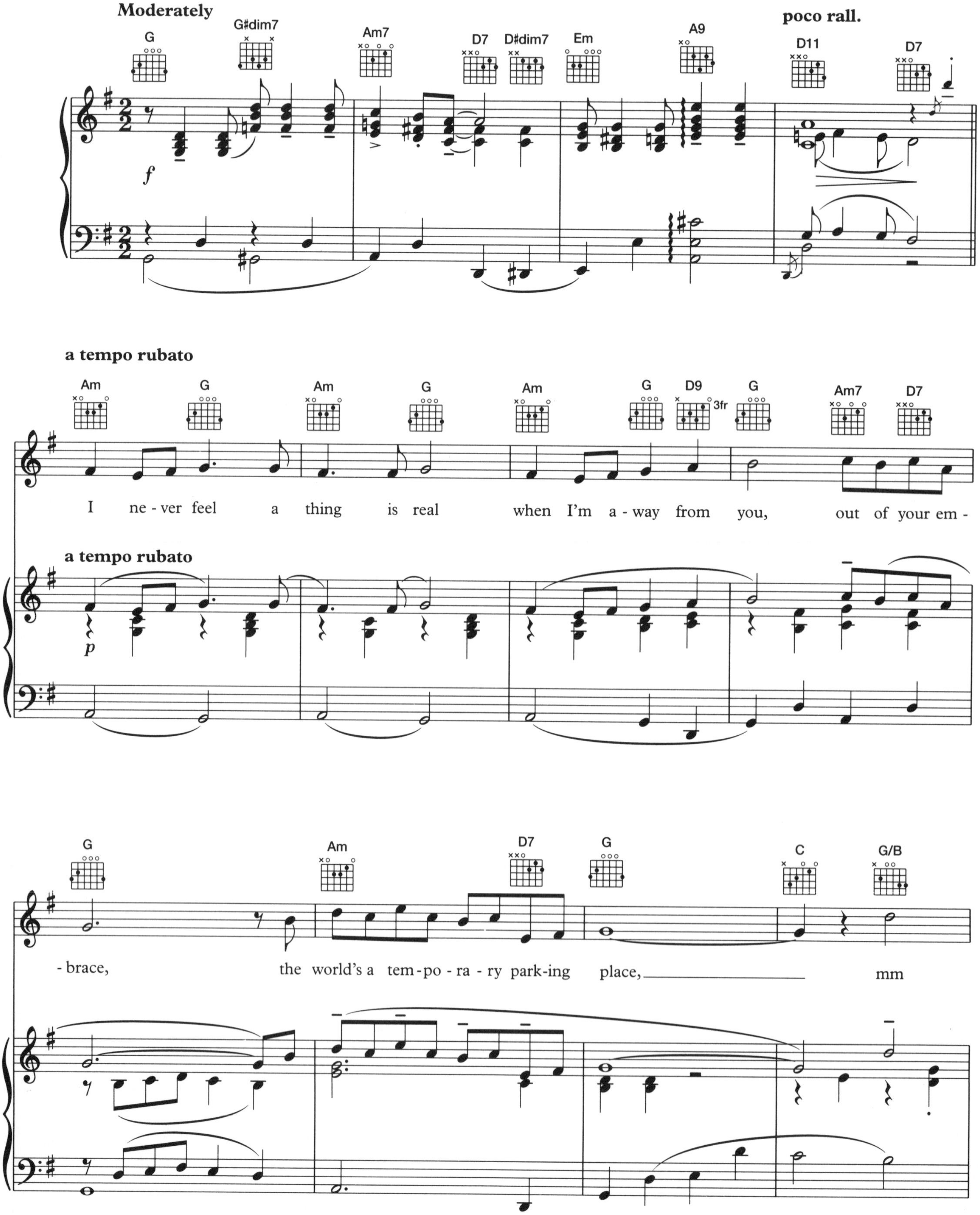

Moderately
G
G#dim7
Am7
D7
D#dim7
Em
A9
poco rall.
D11
D7
f
a tempo rubato
Am
G
Am
G
Am
G
D9
3fr
G
Am7
D7
I ne - ver feel a thing is real when I'm a - way from you, out of your em -
a tempo rubato
p
G
Am
D7
G
C
G/B
- brace, the world's a tem - po - ra - ry park - ing place, mm

Jeepers Creepers

Words by Johnny Mercer
Music by Harry Warren

Let's Call The Whole Thing Off

Music and Lyrics by
George Gershwin and Ira Gershwin

Chords: G Em9 Am7 D13♭9 G Em9

You like po-ta-to and I like po-tah-to, you like to-ma-to and
You like va-nil-la and I like va-nel-la, you, sa's'-pa-ril-la and

Chords: Am7 D13♭9 G G7/F C/E Am7♭5

I like to-mah-to; Po-ta-to, po-tah-to, to-ma-to, to-mah-to!
I sa's'-pa-rel-la; Va-nil-la, va-nel-la, choc' late, straw-b'ry!

Chords: G/B C D11 C/E G C♯m7♭5

Let's call the whole thing off! But oh!

Chords: F♯7 Bm7 E7♭9 Am7 D9 C♯m7♭5

If we call the whole thing off, then we must part. And oh!

Manhattan

Words by Lorenz Hart
Music by Richard Rodgers

Sum-mer jour-neys to Ni-ag-ra And to oth-er plac-es ag-gra-vate all our cares; We'll save our fares; I've a coz-y lit-tle flat in

My Baby Just Cares For Me

Words by Gus Kahn
Music by Walter Donaldson

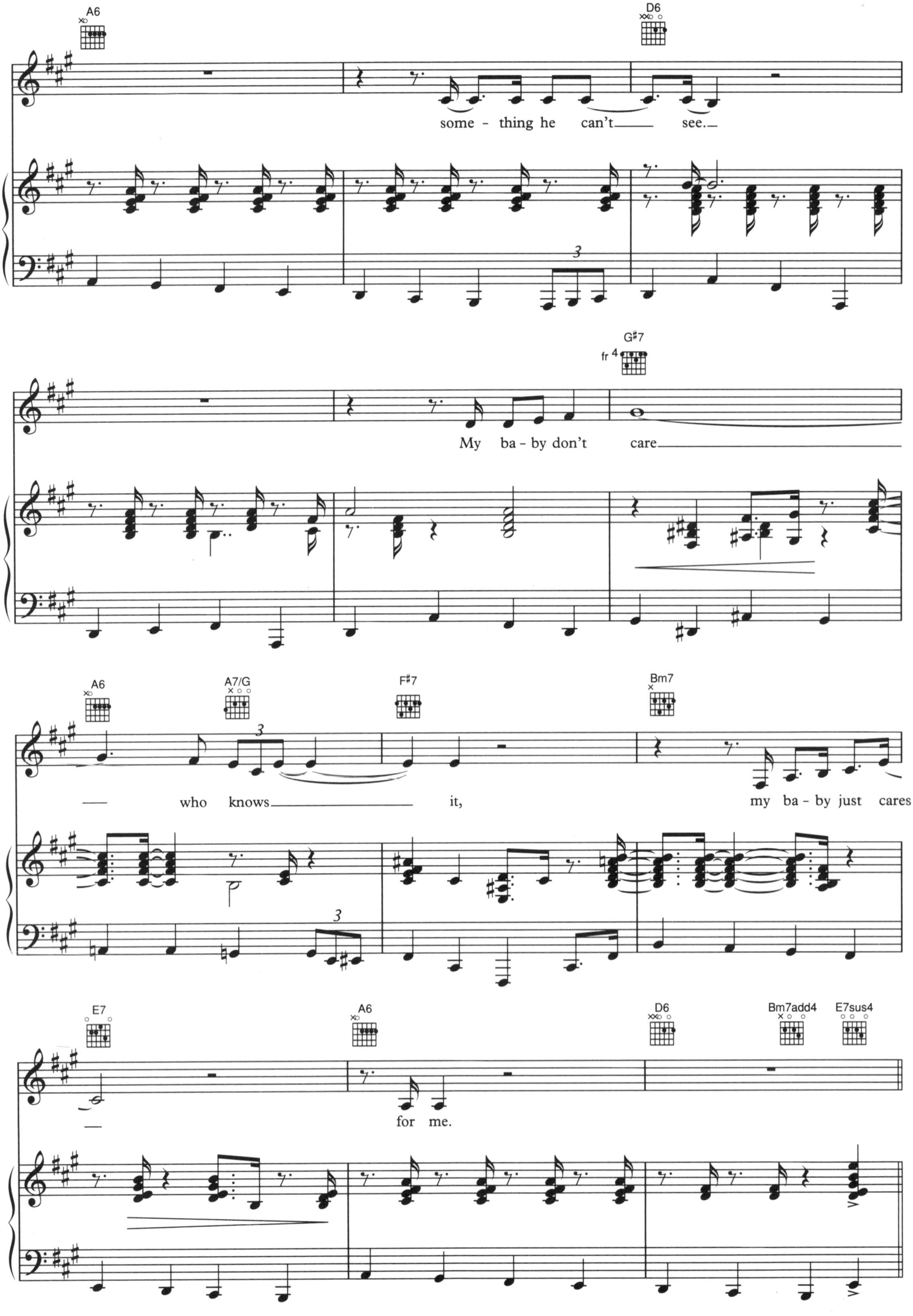
A6
D6
some - thing he can't see.
G♯7
fr 4
My ba - by don't care
A6
A7/G
F♯7
Bm7
who knows it,
my ba - by just cares
E7
A6
D6
Bm7add4
E7sus4
for me.

'Round Midnight

Words and Music by
Cootie Williams and Thelonious Monk

My Funny Valentine

Words by Lorenz Hart
Music by Richard Rodgers

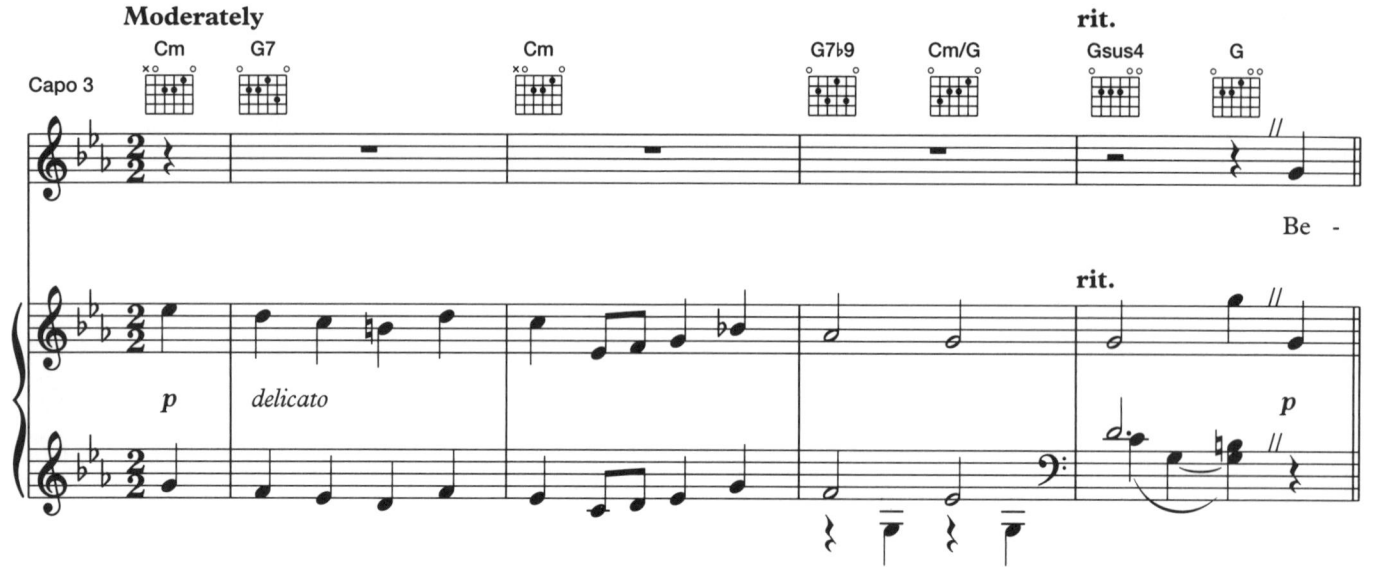

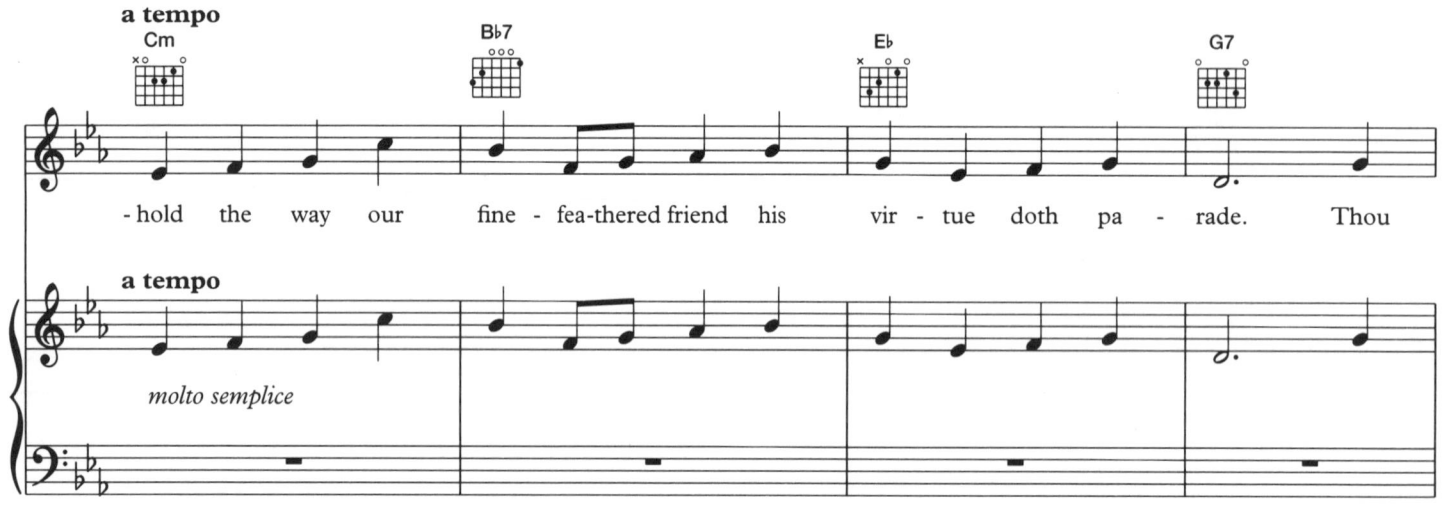

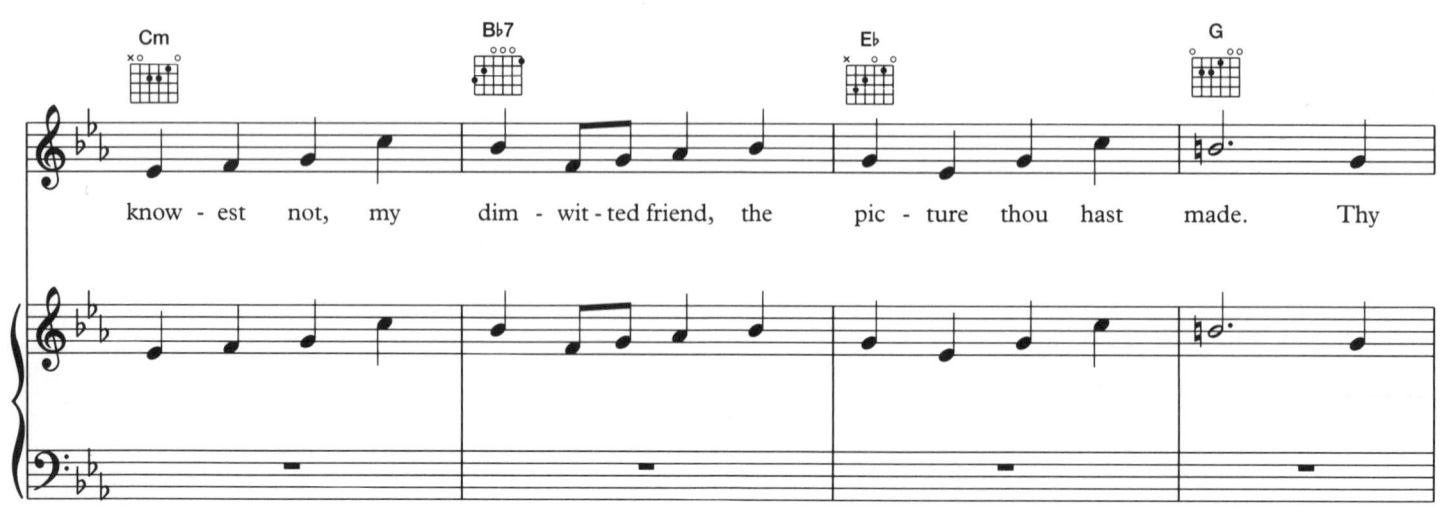

On Green Dolphin Street

Words by Ned Washington
Music by Bronislaw Kaper

Lyrics: It seems like a dream, yet I know it hap-pened. A man, a maid, a kiss and then good-bye. Ro-mance was the theme and we were the play-ers,

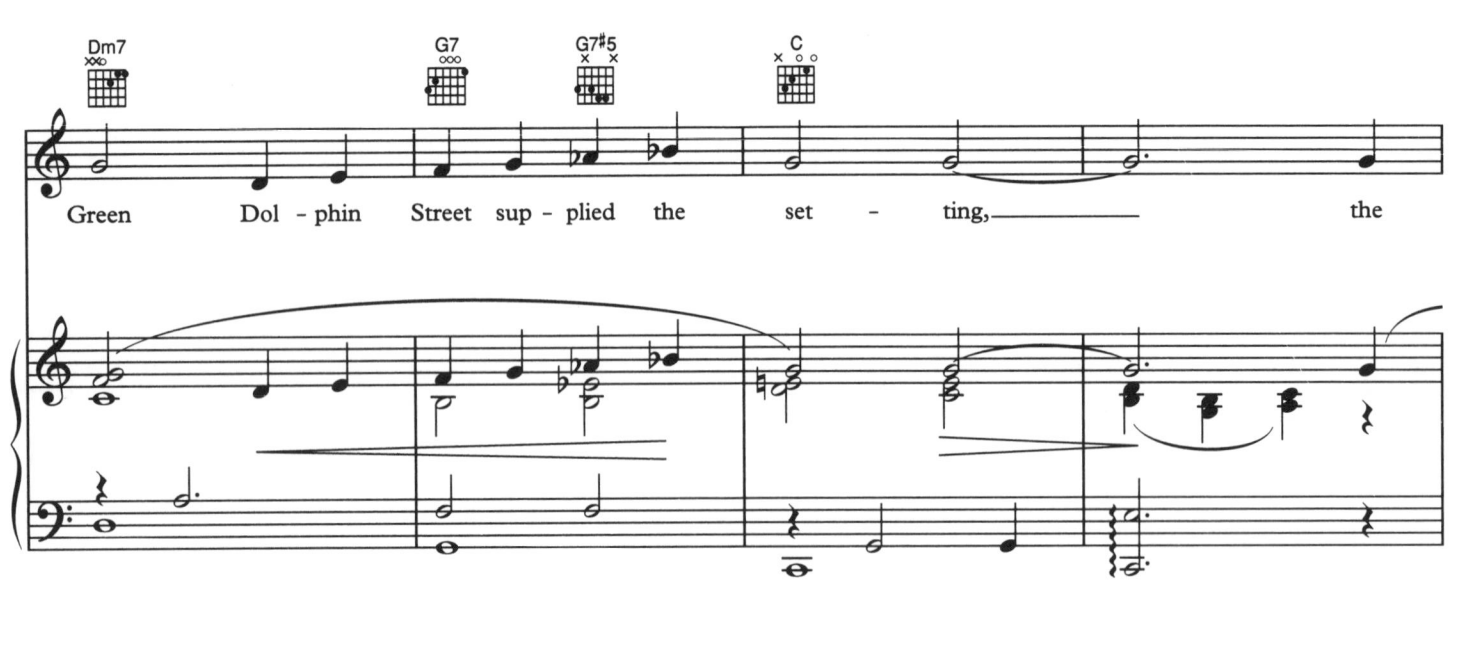

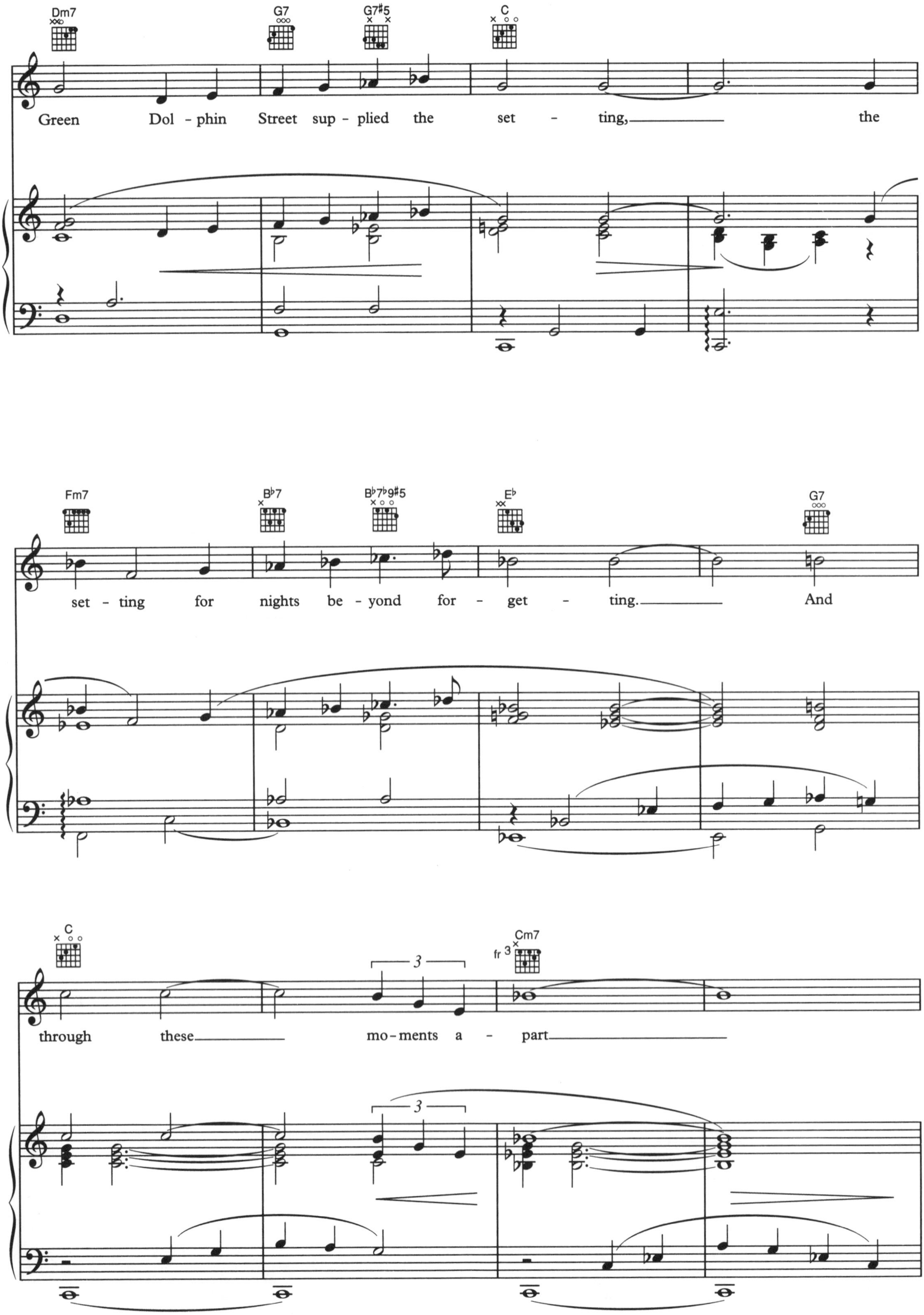

Dm7
G7
G7♯5
C
Green Dol - phin Street sup - plied the set - ting, the
Fm7
B♭7
B♭7♭9♯5
E♭
G7
set - ting for nights be - yond for - get - ting. And
C
Cm7
fr 3
3
through these mo - ments a - part
3

Skylark

Words by Johnny Mercer
Music by Hoagy Carmichael

Stomping At The Savoy

Words and Music by Benny Goodman,
Andy Razaf, Edgar Sampson and Chick Webb

What Is This Thing Called Love?

Words and Music by Cole Porter

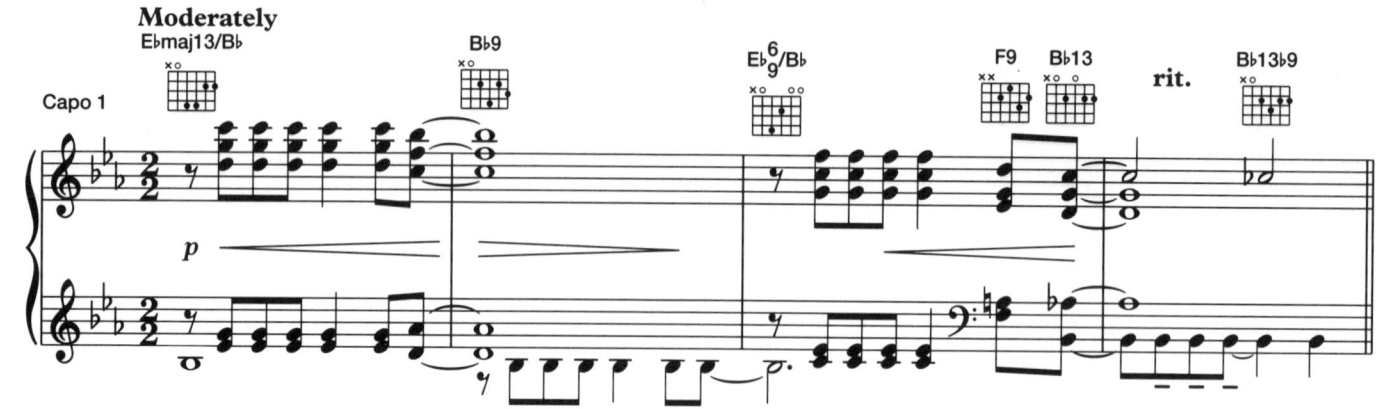

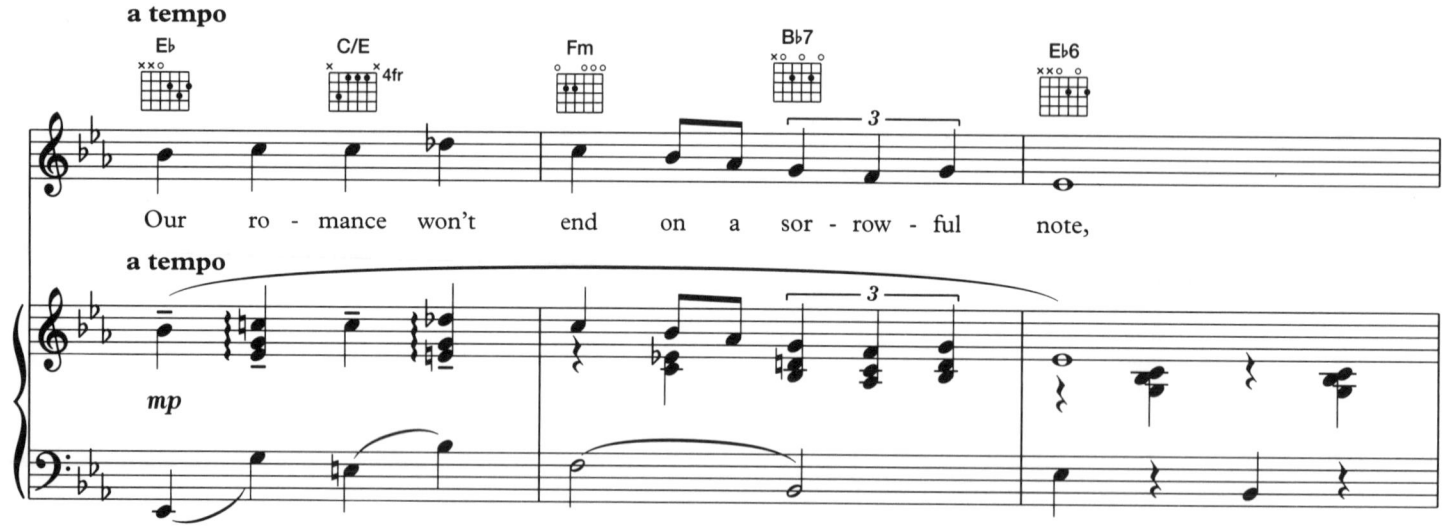

Our ro - mance won't end on a sor - row - ful note,

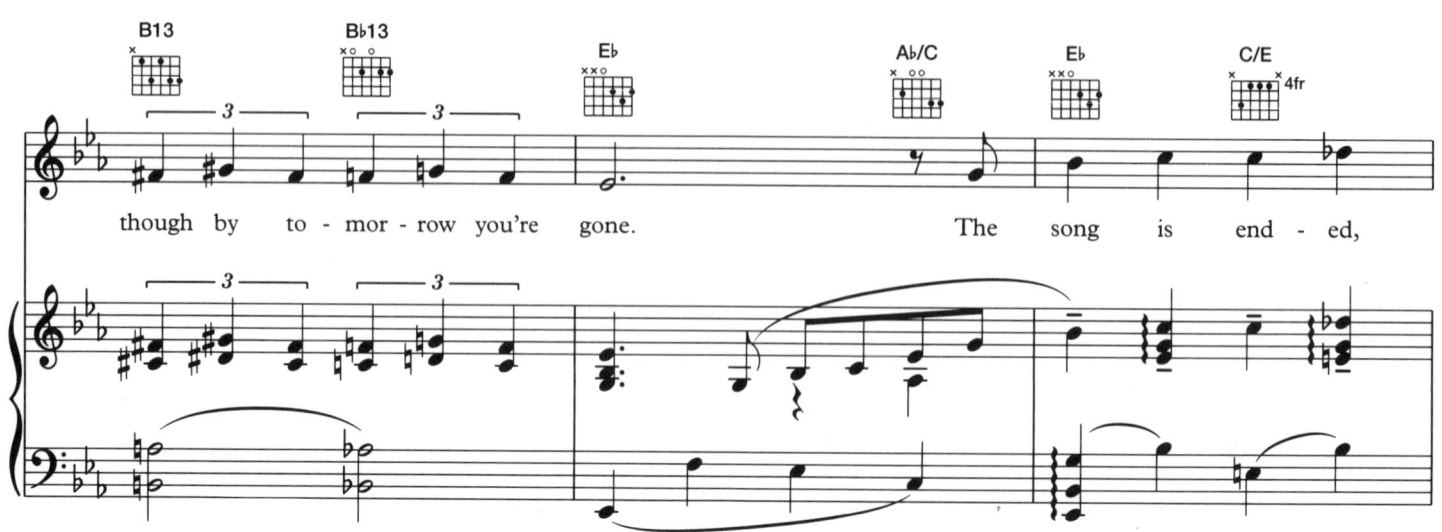

though by to - mor - row you're gone. The song is end - ed,

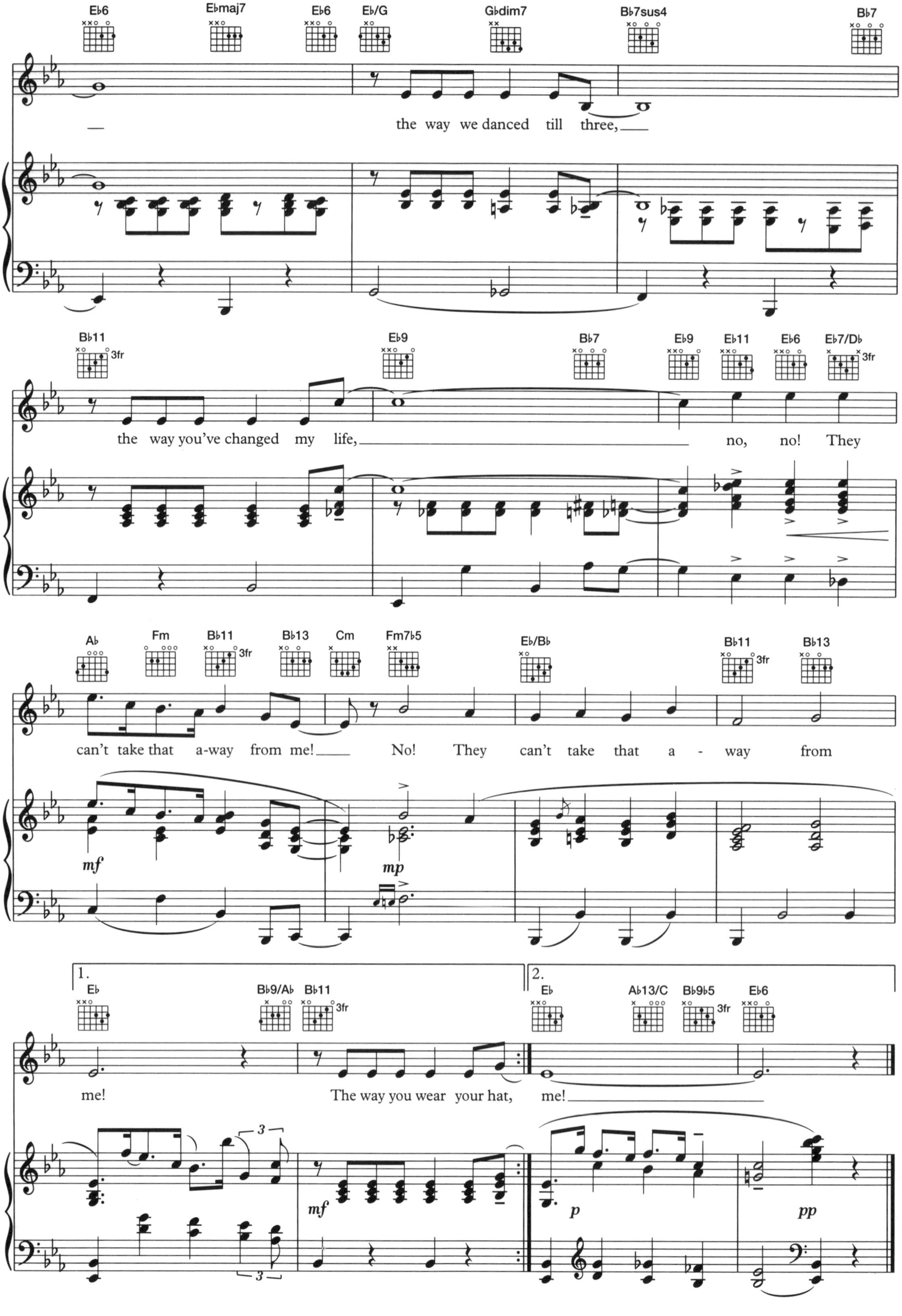
Eb6 Ebmaj7 Eb6 Eb/G Gbdim7 Bb7sus4 Bb7
the way we danced till three,
Bb11 3fr Eb9 Bb7 Eb9 Eb11 Eb6 Eb7/Db 3fr
the way you've changed my life, no, no! They
Ab Fm Bb11 3fr Bb13 Cm Fm7b5 Eb/Bb Bb11 3fr Bb13
can't take that a-way from me! No! They can't take that a - way from
mf mp
1. Eb Bb9/Ab Bb11 3fr
me! The way you wear your hat,
mf
3
2. Eb Ab13/C Bb9b5 3fr Eb6
me!
p pp

They Can't Take That Away From Me

Music and Lyrics by
George Gershwin and Ira Gershwin

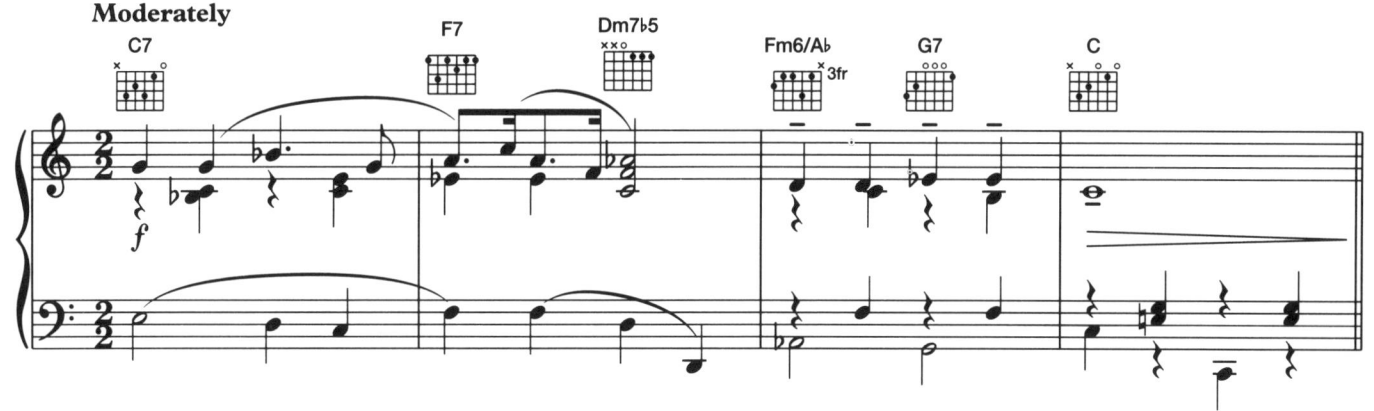

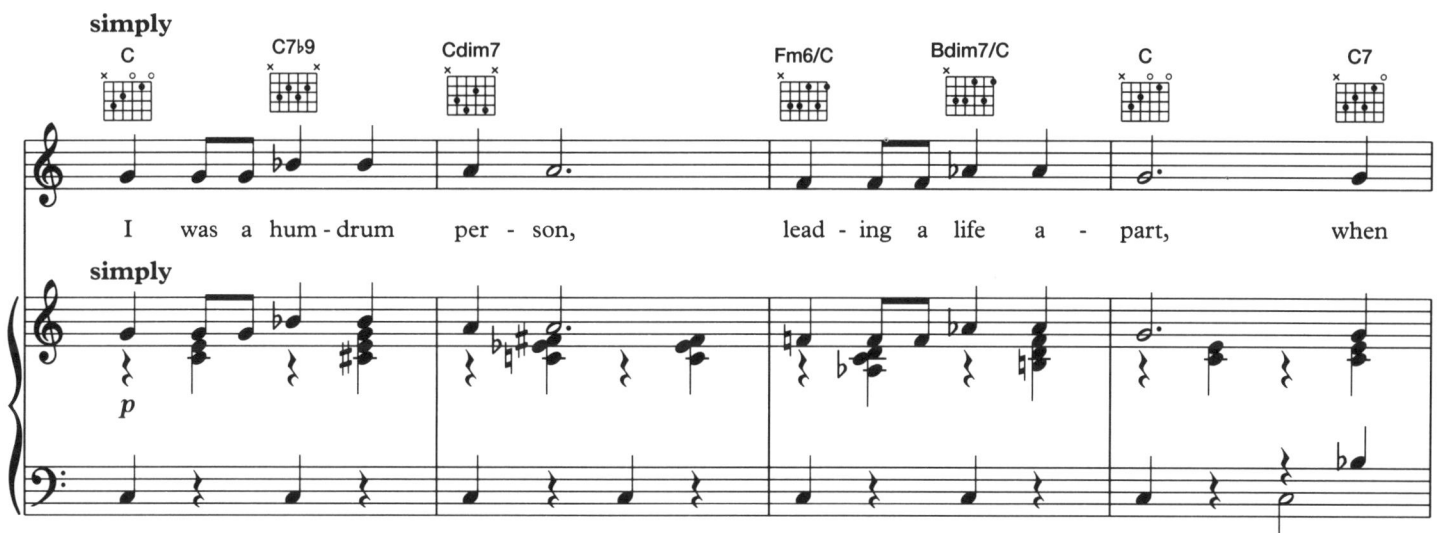

I was a hum-drum per-son, lead-ing a life a-part, when

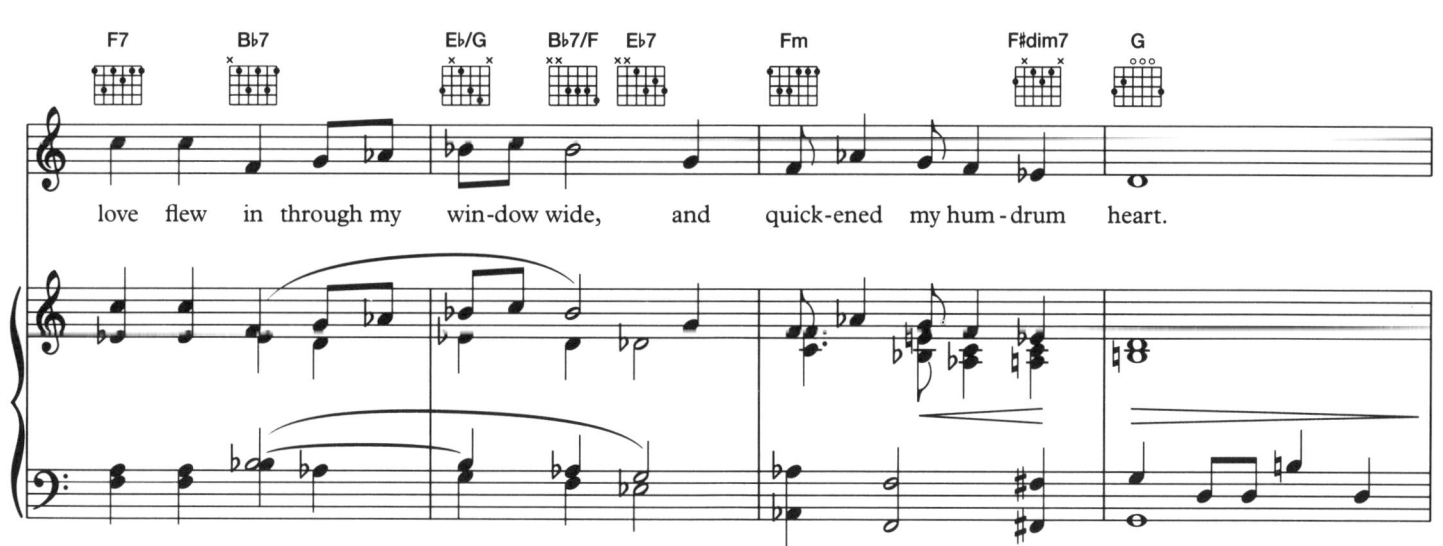

love flew in through my win-dow wide, and quick-ened my hum-drum heart.